Kaplan Publishing are constantly finding new ways to make a difference to your studies and our exciting online resources really do offer something different to students looking for exam success.

This book comes with free MyKaplan online resources so that you can study anytime, anywhere

Having purchased this book, you have access to the following online study materials:

CONTENT	ACCA (including FFA,FAB,FMA)		AAT		FIA (excluding FFA,FAB,FMA)	
	Text	Kit	Text	Kit	Text	Kit
iPaper version of the book	✓	✓	✓	✓	✓	✓
Interactive electronic version of the book	✓					
Progress tests with instant answers	✓		✓			
Mock assessments online			✓	✓		
Material updates	✓	✓	✓	✓	✓	✓
Latest official ACCA exam questions		✓				
Extra question assistance using the signpost icon*		✓				
Timed questions with an online tutor debrief using the clock icon*		✓				
Interim assessment including questions and answers	✓				✓	
Technical articles	✓	✓			✓	✓

* Excludes F1, F2, F3, FFA, FAB, FMA

How to access your online resources

Kaplan Financial students will already have a MyKaplan account and these extra resources will be available to you online. You do not need to register again, as this process was completed when you enrolled. If you are having problems accessing online materials, please ask your course administrator.

If you are already a registered MyKaplan user go to www.MyKaplan.co.uk and log in. Select the 'add a book' feature and enter the ISBN number of this book and the unique pass key at the bottom of this card. Then click 'finished' or 'add another book'. You may add as many books as you have purchased from this screen.

If you purchased through Kaplan Flexible Learning or via the Kaplan Publishing website you will automatically receive an e-mail invitation to MyKaplan. Please register your details using this email to gain access to your content. If you do not receive the e-mail or book content, please contact Kaplan Flexible Learning.

If you are a new MyKaplan user register at www.MyKaplan.co.uk and click on the link contained in the email we sent you to activate your account. Then select the 'add a book' feature, enter the ISBN number of this book and the unique pass key at the bottom of this card. Then click 'finished' or 'add another book'.

Your Code and Information

This code can only be used once for the registration of one book online. This registration and y online content will expire when the final sittings for the examinations covered by this book ha taken place. Please allow one hour from the time you submit your book details for us to proces your request.

GW00500796

Please scratch the film to access your MyKaplan code.

Please be aware that this code is case-sensitive and you will need to include the slashes within the passcode, but not when entering the ISBN. For further technical support, please visit www.MyKaplan.co.uk

AQ2013 Level 3

Prepare Final Accounts for Sole Traders and Partnerships

REVISION KIT

British Library Cataloguing-in-Publication Data

A catalogue record for this book is available from the British Library.

Published by:

Kaplan Publishing UK

Unit 2 The Business Centre

Molly Millar's Lane

Wokingham

Berkshire

RG41 2QZ

ISBN: 978-0-85732-894-6

© Kaplan Financial Limited, 2013

Printed and bound in Great Britain

CONTENTS

Features in this exam kit

In addition to providing a wide ranging bank of real exam style questions, we have also included in this kit:

- Paper specific information and advice on exam technique.

- Our recommended approach to make your revision for this particular subject as effective as possible.

You will find a wealth of other resources to help you with your studies on MyKaplan and AAT websites:

www.mykaplan.co.uk

www.aat.org.uk/

INDEX TO QUESTIONS AND ANSWERS

KAPLAN PUBLISHING

PAPER ENHANCEMENTS

We have added the following enhancements to the answers in this exam kit:

Key answer tips

Some answers include key answer tips to help your understanding of each question.

Tutorial note

Some answers include more tutorial notes to explain some of the technical points in more detail.

EXAM TECHNIQUE

- **Do not skip any of the material** in the syllabus.

- **Read each question** *very* carefully.

- **Double-check your answer** before committing yourself to it.

- Answer **every** question – if you do not know an answer to a multiple choice question or true/false question, you don't lose anything by guessing. Think carefully before you **guess**.

- If you are answering a multiple-choice question, **eliminate first those answers that you know are wrong**. Then choose the most appropriate answer from those that are left.

- **Don't panic** if you realise you've answered a question incorrectly. Getting one question wrong will not mean the difference between passing and failing

Computer-based exams – tips

- Do not attempt a CBA until you have **completed all study material** relating to it.

- On the AAT website there is a CBA demonstration. It is **ESSENTIAL** that you attempt this before your real CBA. You will become familiar with how to move around the CBA screens and the way that questions are formatted, increasing your confidence and speed in the actual exam.

- Be sure you understand how to use the **software** before you start the exam. If in doubt, ask the assessment centre staff to explain it to you.

- Questions are **displayed on the screen** and answers are entered using keyboard and mouse. At the end of the exam, you are given a provisional result.

- In addition to the traditional multiple-choice question type, CBAs will also contain **other types of questions**, such as number entry questions, drag and drop, true/false, pick lists or drop down menus or hybrids of these.

- You need to be sure you **know how to answer questions** of this type before you sit the exam, through practice.

PAPER SPECIFIC INFORMATION

THE EXAM

FORMAT OF THE ASSESSMENT

The assessment consists of five independent tasks (all paper specific) and will normally be assessed by computer-based assessment.

The assessment will cover:

- The process of preparing financial statements and incomplete records
- Producing final accounts for a sole trader
- Understanding the accounting requirements for partnerships and preparing financial statements for partnerships.

Task types will include:

- Calculations
- Completion of ledger accounts
- Completion of pro-forma statements
- Multiple-choice or similar.

Task 1 covers incomplete records and restructuring general ledger accounts.

Task 2 covers missing figures and the process involved in the preparation of financial statements.

Task 3 covers financial statements of sole traders.

Task 4 covers partnership accounting, such as appropriation of profits and losses between partners and admission or retirement of a partner.

Task 5 covers the statement of financial position of a partnership, including partners' capital and current accounts. This may include admission or retirement of a partner.

Time allowed

2 hours

PASS MARK

The pass mark for all AAT CBAs is 70%.

 Always keep your eye on the clock and make sure you attempt all questions!

DETAILED SYLLABUS

The detailed syllabus and study guide written by the AAT can be found at:

www.aat.org.uk/

KAPLAN'S RECOMMENDED REVISION APPROACH

QUESTION PRACTICE IS THE KEY TO SUCCESS

Success in professional examinations relies upon you acquiring a firm grasp of the required knowledge at the tuition phase. In order to be able to do the questions, knowledge is essential.

However, the difference between success and failure often hinges on your exam technique on the day and making the most of the revision phase of your studies.

The **Kaplan textbook** is the starting point, designed to provide the underpinning knowledge to tackle all questions. However, in the revision phase, poring over text books is not the answer.

The Kaplan workbook helps you consolidate your knowledge and understanding and is a useful tool to check whether you can remember key topic areas.

Kaplan pocket notes are designed to help you quickly revise a topic area, however you then need to practise questions. There is a need to progress to exam style questions as soon as possible, and to tie your exam technique and technical knowledge together.

The importance of question practice cannot be over-emphasised.

The recommended approach below is designed by expert tutors in the field, in conjunction with their knowledge of the examiner and the specimen assessment.

You need to practise as many questions as possible in the time you have left.

OUR AIM

Our aim is to get you to the stage where you can attempt exam questions confidently, to time, in a closed book environment, with no supplementary help (i.e. to simulate the real examination experience).

Practising your exam technique is also vitally important for you to assess your progress and identify areas of weakness that may need more attention in the final run up to the examination.

In order to achieve this we recognise that initially you may feel the need to practise some questions with open book help.

Good exam technique is vital.

THE KAPLAN FSTP REVISION PLAN

Stage 1: Assess areas of strengths and weaknesses

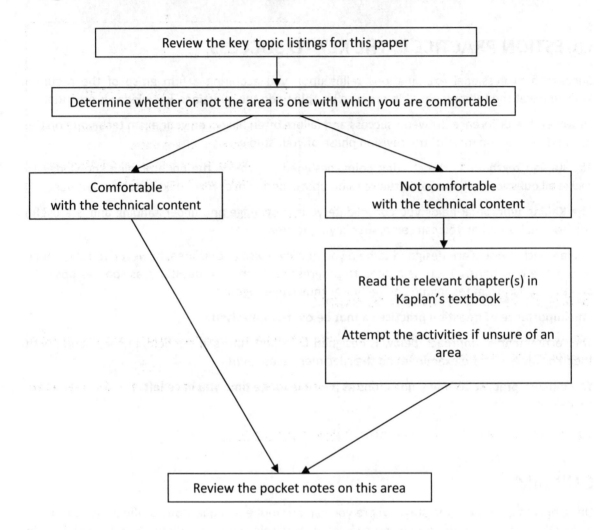

Review the key topic listings for this paper

Determine whether or not the area is one with which you are comfortable

Comfortable
with the technical content

Not comfortable
with the technical content

Read the relevant chapter(s) in
Kaplan's textbook

Attempt the activities if unsure of an
area

Review the pocket notes on this area

Stage 2: Practice questions

Follow the order of revision of topics as presented in this kit and attempt the questions in the order suggested.

Try to avoid referring to text books and notes and the model answer until you have completed your attempt.

Review your attempt with the model answer and assess how much of the answer you achieved.

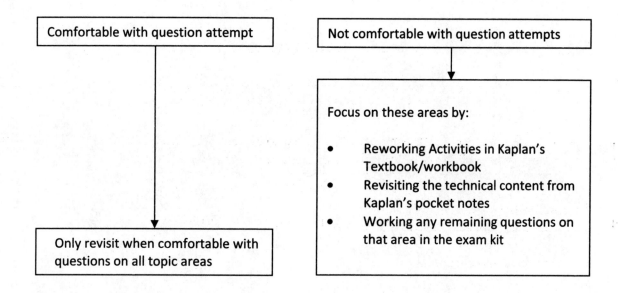

Stage 3: Final pre-exam revision

We recommend that you **attempt at least one two hour mock examination** containing a set of previously unseen exam standard questions.

Attempt the mock CBA online in timed, closed book conditions to simulate the real exam experience

You will find a mock CBA for this subject at www.mykaplan.co.uk

Section 1

PRACTICE QUESTIONS

INCOMPLETE RECORDS

CONTROL ACCOUNTS

1   A CATERING BUSINESS

You are working on the financial statements of a catering business for the year ended 31 May 20X3. You have the following information:

Day book summaries:	Goods £	Sales tax £	Total £
Sales	241,000	48,200	289,200
Purchases	94,000	18,800	112,800

Balances as at:	31 May X2 £	31 May X3 £
Trade receivables	26,000	12,000
Trade payables	21,500	16,800

Further information:	Net £	Sales tax £	Total £
Office expenses	8,000	1,600	9,600

Office expenses are not included in the purchases day book

Bank summary	Dr £		Cr £
Balance b/d	9,620	Travel expenses	14,000
Trade receivables	294,875	Office expenses _VAT_	9,600 _X 6.2_
Interest received	102	Trade payables	115,150
Cash sales (inc sales tax)	18,000	HMRC for sales tax _VAT_	27,525
		Drawings	101,000
		Payroll expenses _VAT_	10,000
		Balance c/d	45,322
	322,597		322,597

_1600_

No VAT on sales.

(a) Using the figures given above, prepare the receivables (sales ledger) control account for the year ended 31 May 20X3. Show clearly discounts as the balancing figure.

Receivables (Sales ledger) control account

Bal (b/d)	26,000	Bank	294,875
SDB	289,200	(c/d)	12,000
		Allowed (c/d)	8,325
			12,000
	315,200		315,200

(b) Find the closing balance for sales tax (VAT) by preparing the sales tax control account for the year ended 31 May 20X3. Use the figures given above. **Note:** The business is not charged sales tax on its travel expenses.

Sales tax control   VAT A/c

POB	18,800	Balance b/d	4,300
Office expense	1,600	SDB	48,200
(c/d)	596,25	Bank	27,525
	20,400		202,400

2 **LOCKE TRADING**

You are working on the financial statements of Locke Trading for the year ended 30 September 20X9. You have the following information:

Day book summaries:	Goods £	Sales tax £	Total £
Sales	195,000	39,000	234,000
Purchases	93,600	18,720	112,320

Balances as at:	30 Sept X8 £	30 Sept X9 £
Trade receivables	16,500	20,625
Trade payables	8,700	12,130

Further information:	Net £	Sales tax £	Total £
Admin expenses	37,000	7,400	44,400
Admin expenses are not included in the purchases day book			

Bank summary	Dr £			Cr £
Balance b/d	8,725	Travel expenses		4,650
Trade receivables	225,000	Office expenses		7,800
Interest received	75	Trade payables		105,200
		Admin expenses		44,400
		Rent		1,500
		HMRC for sales tax		6,450
		Drawings		25,000
		Payroll expenses		13,600
		Balance c/d		25,200
	233,800			233,800

(a) Using the figures given above, prepare the payables (purchase ledger) control account for the year ended 30 September 20X9. Show clearly discounts as the balancing figure.

Payables (Purchase ledger) control account

Bank	105 200	b/d.	8700
Contra	500	PDB	112 320
Bal (c/d)	11630		
	121 020		121 020

(b) Using the figures above find the closing balance for sales tax (VAT) by preparing the sales tax control account for the year ended 30 September 20X9.

Sales tax control

		Balance b/d	2,300

Contra amount of £500
Which has been offset

Contra amount has to be
taken out

3 FIRST POSITION BALLET SUPPLIES

You are working on the financial statements of a business called First Position Ballet Supplies for the year ended 31 December 20X2. You have the following information:

Day book summaries:	Goods £	Sales tax £	Total £
Sales	105,000	21,000	126,000
Purchases	92,000	18,400	110,400

Balances as at:	31 Dec X1 £	31 Dec X2 £
Trade receivables	8,100	11,500
Trade payables	12,400	9,800
Prepayment	300	450
Accrual	250	?

Returns day book summaries:	Net £	Sales tax £	Total £
Sales	19,000	3,800	22,800
Purchases	8,000	1,600	9,600

Bank summary	Dr £		Cr £
Balance b/d	23,400	Electricity expense	5,000
Trade receivables	96,590	Trade payables	?
Interest received	3,810	HMRC	6,100
		Rent	10,000
		Balance c/d	4,200
	123,800		123,800

(a) What is the amount paid through the bank account to trade payables in the year?

£

(b) Using the figures given above (including your answer to part a), prepare the payables (purchase ledger) control account for the year ended 31 December 20X2, showing clearly discounts received as the balancing figure.

Payables (Purchase ledger) control account

(c) The prepayment shown in the schedule is for rent. Using the figures above, calculate the charge to the statement of profit or loss for the year.

Rent expense

(d) The accrual shown above is for electricity. If the electricity charge to the statement of profit or loss for the year is £5,125, calculate the closing accrual.

Electricity expense

4 RELIABLE CARS

You are working on the accounts of Reliable Cars for the year ended 30 September 20X6. You have the following information:

Sales for the year ended 30 September 20X6

- Credit sales amounted to £46,000 net of sales tax
- Cash sales amounted to £212,000 net of sales tax
- All sales are standard rated for sales tax at 20%.

Payments from the bank account for the year ended 30 September 20X6

- Payroll expenses   £48,000
- Administration expenses   £6,400 ignore sales tax
- Vehicle running costs   £192,000 including sales tax at 20%
- Drawings   £41,800
- Sales tax   £17,300

Summary of balances available

Balance as at	30 September 20X5	30 September 20X6
Bank account	5,630	8,140
Trade receivables	4,120	5,710
Sales tax (credit balances)	4,200	4,575

(a)   Calculate the figure for credit sales for entry into the receivables (sales ledger) control account?

£

(b)   Using the figures given above (including your answer to part (a), prepare the sales ledger control account for the year ended 30 September 20X6, showing clearly the receipts paid into the bank as the balancing figure.

Receivables (Sales ledger) control account

(c)   Calculate the cash sales inclusive of sales tax which have been paid into the bank account. All cash sales are banked.

£

(d)   Show a summarised bank account for the year ended 30 September 20X6.

Bank account

5   I.T. SOLUTIONS

I.T. Solutions is owned by Justin Long and started trading on 1 October 20X8. You have been provided with the following summarised bank account, and are required to assist in the preparation of the first set of accounts for the year ended 30 September 20X9

Bank summary for the year ended 30 September 20X9

Capital introduced	16,000	Rent of premises	8,000
Receipts from trade receivables	49,600	Payments to trade payables	18,160
		Travel expenses	4,300
		Administration expenses	3,270
		Drawings	28,000
		Balance c/d	3,870
	65,600		65,600

Additional information:

- Justin transferred his own vehicle into the business on 1 October 20X8. It was valued at £4,000

- On 30 September 20X9, trade receivables owed £6,300

- On 30 September 20X9, trade payables were owed £2,500. Total supplies during the year were £22,000

(a)   Prepare the receivables (sales ledger) control account showing clearly the credit sales as the balancing figure

Receivables (Sales ledger) control account

(b)   Prepare the payables (purchases ledger) control account showing clearly the discounts received as the balancing figure.

Payables (Purchases ledger) control account

(c)   Prepare the opening capital account as at 1 October 20X8, showing clearly all the capital introduced.

Capital account

6   BYRNE

You are working on the financial statements of Byrne who runs a clothing business for the year ended 31 May 20X6. You have the following information:

Day book summaries:	Goods £	Sales tax £	Total £
Sales	270,000	54,000	324,000
Purchases	180,000	36,000	216,000

Balances as at:	31 May X5 £	31 May X6 £
Trade receivables	28,500	24,000
Trade payables	23,750	19,600

Further information:	Net £	Sales tax £	Total £
Office expenses	9,500	1,900	11,400
Office expenses are not included in the purchases day book			

Bank summary	Dr £		Cr £
Trade receivables	325,000	Balance b/d	1,756
Interest received	150	Travel expenses	13,600
Cash sales (inc sales tax)	36,000	Office expenses	11,400
		Trade payables	220,150
		HMRC for sales tax	26,715
		Drawings	45,000
		Payroll expenses	25,000
		Balance c/d	17,529
	361,150		361,150

(a) Using the figures given above, prepare the receivables (sales ledger) control account for the year ended 31 May 20X6. Show clearly sales returns as the balancing figure.

Receivables (Sales ledger) control account

(b) Using the figures given above, prepare the payables (purchase ledger) control account for the year ended 31 May 20X6.

Payables (Purchase ledger) control account

(c) Find the closing balance for sales tax (VAT) by preparing the sales tax control account for the year ended 31 May 20X6. Use the figures given above. **Note:** The business is not charged sales tax on its travel expenses.

		Balance b/d	8,300

THE ACCOUNTING EQUATION/MARGINS AND MARK UPS

7   PERCY

You are given the following information about a sole trader called Percy as at 30 March 20X2:

The value of assets and liabilities were

•	Non-current assets at carrying value	£14,000
•	Bank	£2,500
•	Trade payables	£10,300
•	Opening capital (at 1 April 20X1)	£3,700
•	Drawings for the year	£1,500

There were no other assets or liabilities.

(a)   Calculate the profit for the year ended 30 March 20X2.

£

(b)   Tick the boxes to show whether increases to the account balances would be a debit or credit.

You must choose ONE answer for EACH balance.

	Debit	Credit
Sales		
Prepayment		
Loan		
Accrual		
Trade receivables		

8   GROVER

You are given the following information about a sole trader called Grover as at 1 April 20X8:

The value of assets and liabilities were

- Non-current assets at carrying value   £17,150
- Trade receivables   £4,600
- Allowance for doubtful debts   (£350)
- Prepayments   £200
- Bank overdraft   £600
- Trade payables   £3,750
- Accruals   £325
- Capital   (£11,475)

There were no other assets or liabilities, with the exception of part (a)

(a)   Calculate the long term loan account balance as at 1 April 20X8.

£

(b)   Calculate the accumulated depreciation as at 1 April 20X8 if the non-current asset cost is £75,000.

£

(c)   On 1 June 20X8 a piece of equipment is disposed of and the proceeds received by cheque. Tick the boxes to show what effect this transaction will have on the balances. You must choose ONE answer for EACH line.

	Debit	Credit	No change
Non-current assets cost			
Accumulated depreciation			
Trade receivables			
Trade payables			
Bank			

9 CHIRON

You are given the following information about a sole trader called Chiron as at 31 January 20X5:

The value of assets and liabilities were

- Non-current assets at cost   £10,000
- Trade receivables   £2,000
- Loan   £7,500
- Closing capital (at 31 January 20X5)   £3,500

There were no other assets or liabilities

(a)   Calculate the amount of accumulated depreciation at the year end 31 January 20X5

£

(b)   Chiron sells goods at a mark up of 25%. What would be the gross profit on a sales price of £11,000?

£

10 PARKER

You are given the following information about the business of Parker, a sole trader, as at 1 April 20X8:

The value of assets and liabilities were

- Non-current assets at cost   £25,725
- Non-current asset accumulated depreciation   £8,670
- Trade receivables after allowance for doubtful debts   £4,790
- Prepayments   £190
- Long-term loan   £7,410
- Trade payables   £4,250
- Accruals   £360
- Capital   £10,130

There were no other assets or liabilities, with the exception of part (a)

(a)   Calculate the bank balance as at 1 April 20X8.

£

(b)   Calculate the trade receivables figure as at 1 April 20X8 if the allowance for doubtful debts is £480.

£

(c)   On 1 June 20X8 a piece of equipment is disposed of and the proceeds received in cash. Tick the boxes to show what effect this transaction will have on the balances. You must choose ONE answer for EACH line.

	Debit	Credit	No change
Non-current assets cost			
Accumulated depreciation			
Trade receivables			
Bank balance			
Cash balance			

11   ANNABETH

You are given the following information about a sole trader called Annabeth as at 30 September:

The following balances are available:

Assets and liabilities as at:	30 Sept 20X3 £
Plant and equipment at cost	19,000
Plant and equipment accumulated depreciation	5,600
Inventory at cost	2,890
Cash	560
Bank	2,310
Prepayment for rent	550
Payables for materials	1,720
Accrual for travel expenses	380

Calculate the figure for capital as at 30 September 2003.

£

12   LUKE

Luke sells office equipment. He buys a photocopier for £900.

(a)   What would the selling price be, excluding sales tax, if a 40% mark-up was applied?

(b)   What would the selling price be, excluding sales tax, if the sales margin was 40%?

13 MARK UPPS AND MARGE INNS

Mark Upps and Marge Inns sell kitchen equipment and fittings.

(a) If they buy a gas cooker for £825 excluding sales tax, what would the selling price be, excluding sales tax, if a 40% mark-up was applied?

£

(b) If they buy a gas cooker for £825 excluding sales tax, what would the selling price be, excluding sales tax, if the sales margin was 40%?

£

(c) If they buy a freezer for £250 excluding sales tax, what would the profit be, excluding sales tax, if a 20% mark-up was applied?

£

(d) If they buy a freezer for £250 excluding sales tax, what would the profit be, excluding sales tax, if the sales margin was 20%?

£

(e) If they sell a dishwasher for £455 excluding sales tax, what would the purchase price be, excluding sales tax, if a 30% mark-up was included in the selling price?

£

(f) If they sell a dishwasher for £455 excluding sales tax, what would the purchase price be, excluding sales tax, if a 30% sales margin was included in the selling price?

£

PREPARING FINANCIAL STATEMENTS

STATEMENT OF PROFIT OR LOSS

14 PG TRADING

You have the following trial balance for a sole trader known as PG Trading. All the necessary year end adjustments have been made.

PG Trading		
Trial balance as at 30 September 20X8		
	Dr £	Cr £
Accruals		4,100
Bank	3,500	
Capital		10,100
Closing inventory	19,500	19,500
Depreciation charge	7,100	
Discounts allowed	1,350	

Drawings	11,000	
General expenses	26,100	
Machinery at cost	26,000	
Machinery accumulated depreciation		15,000
Opening inventory	17,700	
Prepayments	4,600	
Purchases	98,000	
Payables (Purchases ledger) control account		32,000
Rent	7,300	
Revenue		170,850
Receivables (Sales ledger) control account	26,400	
Sales tax		5,500
Wages	8,500	
	257,050	257,050

(a)　Prepare a statement of profit or loss for the business for the year ended 30 September 20X8.

PG Trading		
Statement of profit or loss for the year ended 30 September 20X8		
	£	£
Revenue		170850
Opening Inventory	17700	
Purchase	98000	
Closing Inventory	19500	
Cost of goods sold		96200
Gross profit		74650
Less:		
Depreciation Charges	7100	
Discount allowed	1350	
General expense	26100	
Rent	7300	
Wages.	8500	
Total expenses		50350
Profit for the year		24300

(b)   Indicate where the bank balance above (£3,500 debit) should be shown in the financial statements. Choose ONE.

(a)   Non-current assets

(b)   Current assets

(c)   Expenses in the statement of profit or loss

(d)   Current liabilities

15   INVENTORY TRADING

You have the following trial balance for a sole trader known as Inventory Trading. All the necessary year end adjustments have been made.

Inventory Trading		
Trial balance as at 30 September 20X9		
	Dr £	Cr £
Accruals		750
Bank overdraft		1,250
Capital		15,500
Closing inventory	7,850	7,850
Discounts received		900
Sundry payables		1,450
Payables (Purchase ledger) control account		6,800
Depreciation charge	1,600	
Discounts allowed	345	
Irrecoverable debt expense	295	
Drawings	6,500	
Allowance for doubtful debts		840
Equipment at cost	17,500	
Equipment accumulated depreciation		4,500
Prepayments	3,200	
Receivables (Sales ledger) control account	7,800	
Wages	24,000	
Rent	5,250	
Disposal		450
Sales returns	1,500	
Opening Inventory	3,450	
Purchases	125,000	
General expenses	2,950	

Revenue		164,000
Sales tax		2,950
	———	———
	207,240	207,240

(a) Prepare a statement of profit or loss for the business for the year ended 30 September 20X9.

Inventory Trading

Statement of profit or loss for the year ended 30 September 20X9

	£	£
Revenue		162500
Opening Inventory	3450	
Purchases	125000	
Closing Inventory	7850	
Cost of goods sold		120600
Gross profit		41900
Add:		
Prepaid	900	
Disposals	450	
Total Sundry Income		1350
Less:		
Depreciation Charge	1600	
Irrecoverable debt expense	295	
Prepayments		
Wages	24000	
Rent	5250	
General expense	2950	
Discount allowed	345	
Sundry payables	1450	
		35890
Total expenses		84440
Profit for the year		8810

(b) Indicate where the drawings should be shown in the financial statements. Choose ONE.

(i) As an addition to capital

(ii) As a deduction from capital

(iii) As an addition to expenses

(iv) As a deduction from expenses

16 WINSTON PARTNERSHIP

You are preparing the statement of profit or loss for the Winston partnership for the year ended 31 March 20X4. The partners are Julie and Terry.

Winston Trading		
Trial balance as at 31 March 20X4		
	Dr £	Cr £
Accruals		2,500
Bank	3,500	
Capital		4,100
Closing inventory	9,800	9,800
Depreciation charge	800	
Profit on disposal of non-current assets		1,000
Drawings	2,100	
General expenses	8,200	
Machinery at cost	10,500	
Machinery accumulated depreciation		4,300
Opening inventory	9,100	
Prepayments	6,100	
Purchases	38,700	
Payables (Purchases ledger) control account		12,500
Rent	5,900	
Revenue		85,000
Receivables (Sales ledger) control account	18,000	
Sales tax		2,000
Wages	8,500	
	121,200	121,200

Winston Partnership		
Statement of profit or loss for the year ended 31 March 20X4		
	£	£
Revenue		85000
Opening Inventory	9100	
Purchases	38700	
Closing Inventory	9800	
Cost of goods sold		38000
Gross profit		47000
Plus:		
Disposals		1000 .
Less:		
Depreciation Charge	800	
General expense	8200	
Rent	5900	
Wages.	8500	
Total expenses		23400
Profit for the year		24600

17 BALFOUR

You are preparing the statement of profit or loss for the Balfour, a sole trader, for the year ended 31 October 20X7.

Balfour		
Trial balance as at 31 October 20X7		
	Dr £	Cr £
Accruals		1,375
Bank		900
Capital		7,160
Closing inventory	12,500	12,500
Depreciation charge	925	
Disposal of non-current asset		225
Drawings	5,000	
General expenses	9,300	
Machinery at cost	8,000	
Machinery accumulated depreciation		5,200

Opening inventory	13,100	
Prepayments	1,250	
Purchases	68,250	
Purchases ledger control account		11,375
Rent	6,000	
Revenue		108,000
Sales ledger control account	16,500	
Sales tax		6,090
Wages	12,000	
	152,825	152,825

Balfour

Statement of profit or loss for the year ended 31 October 20X7

	£	£
Revenue		108,000
Opening Inventory	13100	
Purchase	68250	
Closing Inventory	12500	
Cost of goods sold		68850
Gross profit		39150
Plus:		
Disposal		225
Less:		
Depreciation Charge	925	
General expense	9300	
Rent	6000	
Wages	12000	
Total expenses		28225
Profit for the year		11150

STATEMENT OF FINANCIAL POSITION

18   R & R TRADING

You have the following trial balance for a partnership known as R & R Trading. All the necessary year end adjustments have been made.

(a)   Prepare a statement of financial position for the business for the year ended 30 September 20X7,

R & R Trading

Trial balance as at 30 September 20X7

	Dr £	Cr £
Accruals		6,000
Bank	5,000	
Capital account partner A		10,000
Capital account partner B		10,000
Closing inventory	11,000	11,000
Depreciation charge	1,800	
Discounts allowed	800	
Current account partner A		2,450
Current account partner B		2,450
General expenses	16,400	
Machinery at cost	15,900	
Machinery accumulated depreciation		5,800
Opening inventory	9,800	
Prepayments	5,100	
Purchases	46,000	
Payables (Purchases ledger) control account		15,900
Rent	200	
Sales		69,000
Receivables (Sales ledger) control account	17,100	
Sales tax		1,500
Wages	5,000	
	134,100	134,100

R & R Trading			
Statement of financial position as at 30 September 20X7			
	£	£	£
Non-current assets	Cost	Depreciation	Carrying Value
Machinery at cost	15900	5800	10100
Current assets			
Inventory		11000	
Trade Rece.		17100	
Bank		5000	
Prepayment		5100	
Current liabilities		38200	38200
Sales Tax.	1500		
Accruals	6000		
Trade P	15900		2043
		23400	
Net current assets			14800
Net assets			24900
Financed by:	A	B	Total
Capital	10000	10000	20000
Current	2450	2450	4900
	12450	12450	24900
		C	

(b) Indicate where the opening inventory in the trial balance (£9,800 debit) should be shown in the financial statements. Choose ONE.

   (i) An increase to cost of sales

   (ii) A reduction to cost of sales

   (iii) A non-current asset

   (iv) Administration expense

19   OSMOND PARTNERSHIP

You are preparing the statement of financial position for the Osmond partnership for the year ended 31 March 20X1. The partners are Aimee and Heather.

All the necessary year end adjustments have been made, except for the transfer of profit to the current accounts of the partners.

Before sharing profits the balances of the partners' current accounts are:

- Aimee   £1,000 credit
- Heather   £ 400 debit

Each partner is entitled to £7,500 profit share.

(a)   Calculate the balance of each partner's current account after sharing profits. Fill in the answers below.

Current account balance: Aimee   £   £ 8500

Current account balance: Heather £   7100

Note: These balances will need to be transferred into the statement of financial position of the partnership which follows.

You have the following trial balance. All the necessary year end adjustments have been made.

(b)   Prepare a statement of financial position for the partnership as at 31 March 20X1. You need to use the partners' current account balances that you have just calculated.

Osmond Partnership		
Trial balance as at 31 March 20X1		
	Dr £	Cr £
Accruals		2,500
Administration expenses	40,000	
Bank	4,100	
Capital – Aimee		29,500
Capital – Heather		42,890
Cash	670	
Closing inventory	20,000	20,000
Current account – Aimee		1,000
Current account – Heather	400	
Depreciation charge	3,600	
Disposal of non-current asset	3,500	
Motor vehicles at cost	39,000	
Motor vehicles accumulated depreciation		18,500

Opening inventory	25,400	
Allowance for doubtful debts		1,200
Change in allowance for doubtful debts	110	
Purchases	83,300	
Payables (Purchases ledger) control account		28,500
Revenue		156,800
Receivables (Sales ledger) control account	78,920	
Selling expenses	5,890	
Sales tax		4,000
Total	304,890	304,890

Osmond Partnership

Statement of financial position as at 31 March 20X1

	£	£	£
Non-current assets	Cost	Depreciation	Carrying Value
Motor Vehicle	39000	18500	20500
Current assets			
Inventory		20000	
Trade R		77720	
Bank		4100	
Cash		670	
		103490	
Current liabilities			
Sales Tax	4000		
Accruals	2500		
Trade P	28500		
		35000	
Net current assets			68490
Net assets			89190
Financed by:	Aimee	Heather	Total
Capital	29500	42890	72390
Current	8500	7100	15600
	38000	49990	87990

20 PERSEPHONE'S

You are preparing the statement of financial position for Persephone's for the year ended 30 June 20X8.

The partners are Tina and Cher.

All the necessary year end adjustments have been made, except for the transfer of profit to the current accounts of the partners.

Before sharing profits the balances of the partners' current accounts are:

- Tina   £3,000 credit
- Cher   £4,500 debit

Each partner is entitled to £4,405 profit share and has taken drawings of £3,250 each.

(a)   Calculate the balance of each partner's current account after sharing profits. Fill in the answers below.

Current account balance: Tina £

Current account balance: Cher £

Note: These balances will need to be transferred into the statement of financial position of the partnership which follows.

You have the following trial balance. All the necessary year end adjustments have been made.

(b)   Prepare a statement of financial position for the partnership as at 30 June 20X8. You need to use the partners' current account balances that you have just calculated.

Persephone's Trial balance as at 30 June 20X8		
	Dr £	Cr £
Accruals		750
Bank Overdraft		1,250
Capital – Tina		8,000
Capital – Cher		9,000
Current – Tina		3,000
Current – Cher	4,500	
Closing Inventory	7,850	7,850
Discounts Received		900
Sundry Payables		1,450
Payables (Purchase ledger) control account		6,800
Depreciation Charge	1,600	
Discounts Allowed	345	
Allowance for Doubtful Debts Increase	295	
Equipment Accumulated Depreciation		4,500
Wages	24,000	

Receivables (Sales ledger) control account	7,800	
Rent	5,250	
Revenue		164,000
Disposal		450
Prepayments	3,200	
Purchases	125,000	
Sales Returns	1,500	
Opening Inventory	3,450	
Equipment at Cost	17,500	
Drawings	6,500	
General Expenses	2,950	
Allowance for Doubtful Debts		840
Sales tax		2,950
	211,740	211,740

Persephone's
Statement of financial position as at 30 June 20X8

	£	£	£
Non-current assets	Cost	Depreciation	Carrying Value
equipment	17500	4500	13000
Current assets			
Inventory		7850	
Trade R		6960	
Prepayments		3200	
		18010	
Current liabilities			
Sales Tax	2950		
Accruals	750		
Trade P	8250		
overdraft	1250	13200	
			4810
Net current assets			17810
Net assets			
Financed by:	Tina	Cher	Total
Capital	8000	9000	17000
Current	4155	3345	7500
	12155	12345	24500

(handwritten margin notes: Trade R, All Doub debt)

PARTNERSHIP ACCOUNTS – CAPITAL AND GOODWILL

21   CELEBRATION CUPCAKES

You have the following information about a partnership:

- The partners are Erica and Hayley, and the partnership sells cupcakes

- Anna was admitted to the partnership on 1 April 20X8 when she introduced £65,000 to the bank account

- Profit share, effective until 31 March 20X8

    - Erica   60%
    - Hayley   40%

- Profit share, effective from 1 April 20X8

    - Erica   40%
    - Hayley   30%
    - Anna   30%

- Goodwill was valued at £40,000 on 31 March 20X8.

- Goodwill is to be introduced into the partners' capital accounts on 31 March and then eliminated on 1 April.

Prepare the capital account for Erica, showing clearly the balance carried down as at 1 April 20X8.

Capital account – Erica

		Balance b/d	10,000
Goodwill c/d	16,000	Goodwill	24,000
	8,000		
	24,000		24,000

22   WYN, FRANCIS AND BILL

Wyn and Francis are in partnership, and have given you the following information.

- Bill was admitted to the partnership on 1 July 20X9 when he introduced £75,000 to the bank account

- Profit share, effective until 30 June 20X9

    - Wyn   60%
    - Francis   40%

- Profit share, effective from 1 July 20X9

    - Wyn   40%
    - Francis   30%
    - Bill   30%

- Goodwill was valued at £45,000 on 30 June 20X9

- Goodwill is to be introduced into the partners' capital accounts on 30 June and then eliminated on 1 July.

(a) Prepare the goodwill account, clearly showing the introduction and elimination of goodwill.

Goodwill

Wyn	18000	Wyn	18000
Francis	27000	Francis	13500
		Bill	13500
	45000		45000

(b) Prepare the capital account for Bill, clearly showing the carried forward balance.

Capital account – Bill

Goodwill	13500	Bank Bill	75000
B c/d			

23 PHIL, GEOFF AND JACK

Phil, Geoff and Jack are in partnership selling dog food.

- Jack retired from the partnership on 30 June 20X5. He has agreed that the partnership will pay what he is due from the bank account in full.

- Profit share, effective until 30 June 20X5

  - Phil   30%
  - Geoff   40%
  - Jack   30%

- Profit share, effective from 1 July 20X5

  - Phil   50%
  - Geoff   50%

- Goodwill was valued at £50,000 on 30 June 20X5

- Goodwill is to be introduced into the partners' capital accounts on 30 June and then eliminated on 1 July.

- At the 30 June 20X5 the partners had the following balances on their capital and current accounts:

  - Phil   £7,000 (capital a/c) and £11,000 (current a/c)
  - Geoff   £8,000 (capital a/c) and £9,000 (current a/c)
  - Jack   £9,000 (capital a/c) and £7,000 (current a/c)

(a)   Prepare the capital account for Jack, showing clearly the transfer from the current account and the amount paid to Jack on his retirement.

Capital account – Jack

		Balance b/d	8,000

(b)   Complete the following sentence by selecting the appropriate account.

If the partnership was unable to pay Jack the balance on his capital account on his retirement, the balance could be transferred to a

1   Non-current asset account

2   Loan account

3   Trade payable account

24   DAN, KIM AND TED

Dan, Kim and Ted are in partnership within the building trade, preparing accounts to the year ended 31 March.

On 30 November 20X4, Dan retired from the partnership. You have the following information about the partnership agreement

- Profit share, effective until 30 November 20X4

  - Dan   40%

  - Kim   30%

  - Ted   30%

- Profit share, effective from 1 December 20X4

  - Kim   50%

  - Ted   50%

- Goodwill was valued at £100,000 on 30 November 20X4

- Goodwill is to be eliminated from the accounts

Prepare the goodwill account for the partnership for the year ended 31 March 20X5, showing clearly the individual transfers to each of the partners' capital accounts.

Goodwill

PARTNERSHIP ACCOUNTS – PROFIT APPROPRIATION AND CURRENT ACCOUNTS

25 RACHAEL, ED AND MATTY

You have the following information about a partnership business:

The financial year ends on 30 June.

- The partners at the beginning of the year were Rachael, Ed and Matty.

- Rachael retired on 31 December 20X8

- Partners' annual salaries

  - Rachael   £18,000

  - Ed   nil

  - Matty   £36,000

- Partners' interest on capital

  - Rachael   £2,000 per full year

  - Ed   £2,000 per full year

  - Matty   £2,000 per full year

- Profit share, effective until 31 December 20X8

  - Rachael   40%

  - Ed   40%

  - Matty   20%

- Profit share, effective from 1 January 20X9

  - Ed   50%

  - Matty   50%

Profit for the year for the year ended 30 June 20X9 was £220,000. You can assume that profits accrue evenly during the year.

Prepare the appropriation account for the partnership for the year ended 30 June 20X9.

Partnership Appropriation account for the year ended 30 June 20X9

	1 Jul 08 – 31 Dec X8 £	1 Jan 09 – 30 Jun X9 £	Total £
Profit for the year			
Salaries:			
Rachael			
Ed			
Matty			
Interest on capital:			
Rachael			
Ed			
Matty			
Profit available for distribution			

Profit share:			
Rachael			
Ed			
Matty			
Total profit distributed			

26 NYAH, SHAUNA AND MOLLIE

You have the following information about a partnership business:

- The financial year ends on 31 March.

- The partners at the beginning of the year were Nyah, Shauna and Mollie.

- Mollie retired on 31 December 20X9.

- Partners' annual salaries

    – Nyah   £25,000

    – Shauna   £19,000

    – Mollie   nil

- Partners' interest on capital

    – Nyah   £1,100 per full year

    – Shauna   £1,100 per full year

    – Mollie   £1,100 per full year

- Profit share, effective until 31 December 20X9
  - Nyah   40%
  - Shauna   40%
  - Mollie   20%
- Profit share, effective from 1 January 20Y0
  - Nyah   75%
  - Shauna   25%

Profit for the year for the year ended 31 March 20Y0 was £70,000. You can assume that profits accrued evenly during the year.

Prepare the appropriation account for the partnership for the year ended 31 March 20Y0.

Partnership Appropriation account for the year ended 31 March 20Y0

	1 Apr X9 – 31 Dec X9 £	1 Jan Y0 – 31 Mar Y0 £	Total £
Profit for the year			
Salaries:			
Nyah			
Shauna			
Mollie			
Interest on capital:			
Nyah			
Shauna			
Mollie			
Profit available for distribution			

Profit share:			
Nyah			
Shauna			
Mollie			
Total profit distributed			

27   EDWARD, JAKE AND BELLA

This task is about partnership accounts. You have the following information about a partnership business:

- The financial year ends on 31 December.

- The partners at the beginning of the year were Edward, Jake and Bella.

- Jake left the partnership on 30 April 20X0.

- Partners' annual salaries

    - Edward   £30,000

    - Jake   nil

    - Bella   £21,000

- Partners' interest on capital

    - Edward   £3,000 per full year

    - Jake   £3,000 per full year

    - Bella   £3,000 per full year

- Profit share, effective until 30 April 20X0

    - Edward   50%

    - Jake   20%

    - Bella   30%

- Profit share, effective from 1 May 20X0

    - Edward   60%

    - Bella   40%

Profit for the year for the year ended 31 December 20X0 was £360,000. You can assume that profits accrued evenly during the year.

Prepare the appropriation account for the partnership for the year ended 31 December 20X0.

Partnership Appropriation account for the year ended 31 December 20X0

	1 Jan X0 – 30 Apr X0 £	1 May X0 – 31 Dec X0 £	Total £
Profit for the year			
Salaries:			
Edward			
Jake			
Bella			
Interest on capital:			
Edward			
Jake			
Bella			
Profit available for distribution			

Profit share:			
Edward			
Jake			
Bella			
Total profit distributed			

28 GARY, MARK AND ROBBIE

Gary, Mark and Robbie are in partnership, preparing accounts to the year ended 30 June. You are given the following information:

- The financial year ends on 30 June.

- Partners' annual salaries

  - Gary   £18,000

  - Mark   nil

  - Robbie   £36,000

- Partners' capital account balances as at 30 June 20X9

  - Gary   £100,000

  - Mark   £60,000

  - Robbie   £75,000

- Interest on capital is charged at 5% per annum on the capital account balance at the end of the financial year.

- The partners share the remaining profit of £80,000 as follows:

  - Gary   40%

  - Mark   40%

  - Robbie   20%

- Partners' drawings for the year

  - Gary   £34,000

  - Mark   £30,000

  - Robbie   £58,000

Prepare the current accounts for the partners for the year ended 30 June 20X9, showing clearly the balances carried down.

Current accounts

	Gary £	Mark £	Robbie £		Gary £	Mark £	Robbie £
				Balance b/d	2,000	1,500	250

29 JOHN, JACKIE AND TEGAN

John, Jackie and Tegan are in partnership, producing accounts to the year ended 30 June. You are given the following information:

- Partners' annual salaries

  - John   £11,000

  - Jackie   £16,500

  - Tegan   nil

- Partners' capital account balances as at 30 June 20X8

  - John   £47,500

  - Jackie   £56,000

  - Tegan   £56,000

- Interest on capital is charged at 4% per annum on the capital account balance at the end of the financial year.

- The partners share the **remaining** profit of £75,000 as follows:
  - John   35%
  - Jackie   45%
  - Tegan   20%
- Partners' drawings for the year
  - John   £18,000
  - Jackie   £35,000
  - Tegan   £12,750

Prepare the current accounts for the partners for the year ended 30 June 20X8. Show clearly the balances carried down.

Current accounts

	John £	Jackie £	Tegan £		John £	Jackie £	Tegan £
Balance b/d	750			Balance b/d		1,900	600

30   LOUIS, CHERYL AND SIMON

Louis, Cheryl and Simon are in partnership producing accounts to the year ended 31 December. You are given the following information:

- Partners' annual salaries
  - Louis   £30,000
  - Cheryl   nil
  - Simon   £21,000
- Partners' capital account balances as at 31 December 20X9
  - Louis   £50,000
  - Cheryl   £50,000
  - Simon   £20,000
- Interest on capital is charged at 2% per annum on the capital account balance at the end of the financial year.

- The partners share the remaining profit of £60,000 as follows:

    - Louis   50%

    - Cheryl   20%

    - Simon   30%

- Partners' drawings for the year

    - Louis   £25,000

    - Cheryl   £10,200

    - Simon   £31,000

Prepare the current accounts for the partners for the year ended 31 December 20X9. Show clearly the balances carried down.

Current accounts

	Louis £	Cheryl £	Simon £		Louis £	Cheryl £	Simon £
				Balance b/d	3,500	1,800	1,000

31   DEREK, JIN AND AHMED

Derek, Jin and Ahmed are in business together sharing profits in the ratio 3:3:4 after providing for salaries for Derek and Jin of £20,000 and £24,000 respectively. The partners each receive interest of 8% per annum on their capital balances and pay interest of 10% on their drawings. The profit for the year to 31 March 20X8 is £254,000 before providing for salaries or interest.

The partners' capital balances and drawings are as follows:

	Capital balance £	Drawings on 1 April 20X7 £
Derek	100,000	46,000
Jin	90,000	38,000
Ahmed	132,000	48,000
Total	322,000	132,000

Prepare the appropriation account for the partnership for the year ended 31 March 20X8.

Partnership Appropriation account for the year ended 31 March 20X8:

	£	£
Profit for the year		
Salaries:		
Derek		
Jin		
Ahmed		
Interest on capital:		
Derek		
Jin		
Ahmed		
Interest on drawings:		
Derek		
Jin		
Ahmed		
Profit available for distribution		
Profit share:		
Derek		
Jin		
Ahmed		
Total profit distributed		

32 FRED AND JIM

Fred and Jim are in partnership sharing profits equally and compiling financial statements to 31 December each year. They are both paid a salary of £20,000 each year. They receive 5% interest on their capital balances and pay interest of 10% per annum on their drawings.

Fred has £56,000 invested in the partnership and Jim has £125,000. Fred took £25,000 out of the business on the 1 April 20X8 and a further £12,000 on 1 September 20X8. The profit for the year ended 31 December 20X8 is £182,225 before providing for salaries and interest.

Prepare the appropriation account for the partnership for the year ended 31 December 20X8.

Partnership Appropriation account for the year ended 31 December 20X8:

	£	£
Profit for the year		
Salaries:		
Fred		
Jim		
Interest on capital:		
Fred		
Jim		
Interest on drawings:		
Fred (W)		
Jim		
Profit available for distribution		
Profit share:		
Fred		
Jim		
Total profit distributed		

UNDERPINNING KNOWLEDGE

33 SHORT FORM QUESTIONS

1 A trial balance guarantees there are no errors in the accounting records.

(a) True

(b) False

2 Which of the following is best described as a non-current asset. Choose ONE answer.

(a) A car purchased for resale by a car dealer

(b) A positive bank account (debit)

(c) A car for use by the company salesman

(d) An insurance invoice covering the following 12 month period

3   Which of the following is best described as a current liability? Choose ONE answer.

(a)   An item of inventory that will be sold in the next couple of months

(b)   A delivery van that will be sold next week

(c)   A loan that will be paid back to the bank in the next few months

(d)   A sales invoice for goods sold to a customer that will be paid in the next month

4   When extending the trial balance, if the debit column of the statement of profit or loss is £125,000 and the credit column is £137,000, what entry would be required?

(a)   None

(b)   Dr Statement of profit or loss £12,000 / Cr statement of financial position £12,000

(c)   Dr Statement of profit or loss £12,000

(d)   Dr statement of financial position £12,000 / Cr Statement of profit or loss £12,000

5   Referring back to question 4, is this a profit or a loss?

(a)   Profit

(b)   Loss

6   For each of the transactions below, tick whether the account balance would be debited, credited or would not change. Choose ONE answer for each line.

(a)   A sole trader makes a credit sale (ignore sales tax)

	Debit	Credit	No change
Revenue			
Loan			
Non-current assets			
Trade receivables			

(b)   A sole trader decides to write off an irrecoverable debt

	Debit	Credit	No change
Trade payables			
Inventory			
Irrecoverable debt expense			
Trade receivables			

(c)   A sole trader purchases a new computer on credit for use in the business

	Debit	Credit	No change
Discount allowed			
Sundry payables			
Non-current assets			
Inventory			

Section 2

ANSWERS TO PRACTICE QUESTIONS

INCOMPLETE RECORDS

CONTROL ACCOUNTS

1   A CATERING BUSINESS

Receivables (Sales ledger) control account

Balance b/d	26,000		
SDB	289,200	Bank	294,875
		Discount allowed	8,325
		Balance c/d	12,000
	315,200		315,200

Sales tax control

PDB	18,800	Balance b/d	4,300
Office expenses	1,600	SDB	48,200
Bank	27,525	Cash sales	3,000
Balance c/d	7,575		
	55,500		55,500

2   LOCKE TRADING

Payables (Purchases ledger) control account

Bank	105,200	Balance b/d	8,700
Discounts received	3,690	PDB	112,320
Balance c/d	12,130		
	121,020		121,020

Sales tax control

PDB	18,720	Balance b/d	2,300
Admin expenses	7,400	SDB	39,000
Bank	6,450		
Balance c/d	8,730		
	41,300		41,300

3 FIRST POSITION BALLET SUPPLIES

(a) £98,500

(b) **Payables (Purchases ledger) control account**

Bank	98,500	Balance b/d	12,400
PRDB	9,600	PDB	110,400
Discount received	4,900		
Balance c/d	9,800		
	122,800		122,800

(c) **Rent expense**

Balance b/d	300	Profit or loss	9,850
Bank	10,000	Balance c/d	450
	10,300		10,300

(d) **Electricity expense**

Bank	5,000	Balance b/d	250
Balance c/d	375	Profit or loss	5,125
	5,375		5,375

4   RELIABLE CARS

(a)   £55,200

(b)   **Sales ledger control account**

Balance b/d	4,120	Bank	53,610
Credit sales	55,200	Balance c/d	5,710
	59,320		59,320

(c)   £254,400

(d)   **Bank account**

Balance b/d	5,630	Payroll expenses	48,000
SLCA	53,610	Administration expenses	6,400
Cash sales	254,400	Vehicle running costs	192,000
		Drawings	41,800
		Sales tax	17,300
		Balance c/d	8,140
	313,640		313,640

5   I.T. SOLUTIONS

(a)   **Receivables (Sales ledger) control account**

		Bank	49,600
		Balance c/d	6,300
Credit sales	55,900		
	55,900		55,900

(b)   **Payables (Purchases ledger) control account**

Bank	18,160	Purchases	22,000
Balance c/d	2,500		
Discounts received	1,340		
	22,000		22,000

(c)   **Capital account**

		Bank	16,000
		Motor vehicle cost	4,000
Balance c/d	20,000		
	20,000		20,000

6   BYRNE

(a)   **Receivables (Sales ledger) control account**

Balance b/d	28,500	Bank	325,000
SDB	324,000	Sales returns	3,500
		Balance c/d	24,000
	352,500		352,500

(b)   **Payables (Purchase ledger) control account**

Bank	220,150	Balance b/d	23,750
Balance c/d	19,600	PDB	216,000
	239,750		239,750

(c)   **Sales tax control**

PDB	36,000	Balance b/d	8,300
Office expenses	1,900	SDB	54,000
Bank	26,715	Cash sales	6,000
Balance c/d	3,685		
	68,300		68,300

THE ACCOUNTING EQUATION/MARGINS AND MARK UPS

7   PERCY

(a)   £4,000

(b)

	Debit	Credit
Sales		✓
Prepayment	✓	
Loan		✓
Accrual		✓
Trade receivables	✓	

8   GROVER

(a)   £5,450

(b)   £57,850

(c)

	Debit	Credit	No change
Non-current asset cost		✓	
Accumulated depreciation	✓		
Trade receivables			✓
Trade payables			✓
Bank	✓		

9   CHIRON

(a)   £1,000

(b)   £2,200

10   PARKER

(a)   £115

(b)   £5,270

(c)

	Debit	Credit	No change
Non-current asset cost		✓	
Accumulated depreciation	✓		
Trade receivables			✓
Bank balance			✓
Cash balance	✓		

11 ANNABETH

£17,610

12 LUKE

(a) 900 + 40% = £1,260

(b) 900 × 100/60 = £1,500

13 MARK UPPS AND MARGE INNS

(a) £825 + 40% = £1,155

(b) £825 × 100/60 = £1,375

(c) £250 × 20% = £50

(d) £250 × 100/80 × 20% = £62.50

(e) £455 / 1.3 = £350

(f) £455 × 100/70 = £318.50

PREPARING FINANCIAL STATEMENTS

STATEMENT OF PROFIT OR LOSS

14 PG TRADING

PG Trading Statement of profit or loss for the year ended 30 September 20X8	£	£
Revenue		170,850
Opening inventory	17,700	
Purchases	98,000	
Closing inventory	19,500	
Cost of goods sold		96,200
Gross profit		74,650
Less:		
Depreciation charge	7,100	
Discounts allowed	1,350	
General expenses	26,100	
Rent	7,300	
Wages	8,500	
Total expenses		50,350
Net profit		24,300

(b) Current assets

15 INVENTORY TRADING

Inventory Trading		
Statement of profit or loss for the year ended 30 September 20X9		
	£	£
Revenue (W)		162,500
Opening inventory	3,450	
Purchases	125,000	
Closing inventory	7,850	
Cost of goods sold		120,600
Gross profit		41,900
Add:		
Discounts received	900	
Disposal	450	
Total Sundry Income		1,350
Less:		
Depreciation charge	1,600	
Discounts allowed	345	
General expenses	2,950	
Rent	5,250	
Irrecoverable bad debt expense	295	
Wages	24,000	
Total expenses		34,440
Net profit		8,810

Working:

	£
Revenue per TB	164,000
Sales returns per TB	(1,500)
	─────
	162,500
	─────

(b) As a deduction from capital

16   WINSTON PARTNERSHIP

Winston Partnership

Statement of profit or loss for the year ended 31 March 20X4

	£	£
Revenue		85,000
Opening inventory	9,100	
Purchases	38,700	
Closing inventory	9,800	
Cost of goods sold		38,000
Gross profit		47,000
Plus:		
Profit on disposal		1,000
Less:		
Depreciation charge	800	
General expenses	8,200	
Rent	5,900	
Wages	8,500	
Total expenses		23,400
Net profit		24,600

17   BALFOUR

Balfour

Statement of profit or loss for the year ended 31 October 20X7

	£	£
Revenue		108,000
Opening inventory	13,100	
Purchases	68,250	
Closing inventory	12,500	
Cost of goods sold		68,850
Gross profit		39,150
Plus:		
Profit on disposal		225
Less:		
Depreciation charge	925	
General expenses	9,300	
Rent	6,000	
Wages	12,000	
Total expenses		28,225
Net profit		11,150

STATEMENT OF FINANCIAL POSITION

18   R & R TRADING

R & R Trading			
Statement of financial position as at 30 September 20X7			
	£	£	£
Non-current assets	Cost	Depreciation	Carrying Value
Machinery	15,900	5,800	10,100
Current assets			
Inventory		11,000	
Trade receivables		17,100	
Bank		5,000	
Prepayments		5,100	
		38,200	
Current liabilities			
Trade payables	15,900		
Accruals	6,000		
Sales tax	1,500		
		23,400	
Net current assets			14,800
Net assets			24,900
Financed by:	A	B	Total
Capital account	10,000	10,000	20,000
Current account	2,450	2,450	4,900
	12,450	12,450	24,900

(b)   An increase to cost of sales

19   OSMOND PARTNERSHIP

Current account balance: Aimee   £8,500 (credit)

Current account balance: Heather   £7,100 (credit)

Osmond Partnership

Statement of financial position as at 31 March 20X1

	£	£	£
Non-current assets	Cost	Depreciation	Carrying Value
Motor vehicles	39,000	18,500	20,500
Current assets			
Inventory		20,000	
Trade receivables (W)		77,720	
Bank		4,100	
Cash		670	
		102,490	
Current liabilities			
Trade payables	28,500		
Sales tax	4,000		
Accruals	2,500		
		35,000	
Net current assets			67,490
Net assets			87,990
Financed by:	Aimee	Heather	Total
Capital accounts	29,500	42,890	72,390
Current accounts	8,500	7,100	15,600
	38,000	49,990	87,990

Working:

	£
Trade receivables per TB	78,920
Allowance for doubtful debt	(1,200)
	77,720

20 PERSEPHONE'S

Current account balance: Tina   £4,155 (credit)

Current account balance: Cher   (£3,345) (debit)

Persephone's Statement of financial position as at 30 June 20X8			
	£	£	£
Non-current assets	Cost	Depreciation	Carrying Value
Equipment	17,500	4,500	13,000
Current assets			
Inventory		7,850	
Trade receivables (W1)		6,960	
Prepayments		3,200	
		18,010	
Current liabilities			
Payables (W2)	8,250		
Sales tax	2,950		
Accruals	750		
Overdraft	1,250		
		13,200	
Net current assets			4,810
Net assets			17,810
Financed by:	Tina	Cher	Total
Capital accounts	8,000	9,000	17,000
Current accounts	4,155	(3,345)	810
	12,155	5,655	17,810

Working:

	£
Trade receivables per TB	7,800
Allowance for doubtful debt	(840)
	6,960
PLCA	6,800
Sundry payables	1,450
	8,250

PARTNERSHIP ACCOUNTS – CAPITAL AND GOODWILL

21 CELEBRATION CUPCAKES

Capital account – Erica

Goodwill	16,000	Balance b/d	10,000
Balance c/d	18,000	Goodwill	24,000
	34,000		34,000

22 WYN, FRANCIS AND BILL

Goodwill

Capital – Wyn	27,000	Capital – Wyn	18,000
Capital – Francis	18,000	Capital – Francis	13,500
		Capital – Bill	13,500
	45,000		45,000

Capital account – Bill

Goodwill	13,500	Bank	75,000
Balance c/d	61,500		
	75,000		75,000

23 PHIL, GEOFF AND JACK

Capital account – Jack

Bank	31,000	Balance b/d	9,000
		Goodwill	15,000
		Current account	7,000
	31,000		31,000

2   Loan account

24 DAN, KIM AND TED

Goodwill

Capital – Dan	40,000	Capital – Kim	50,000
Capital – Kim	30,000	Capital – Ted	50,000
Capital – Ted	30,000		
	100,000		100,000

PARTNERSHIP ACCOUNTS – PROFIT APPROPRIATION AND CURRENT ACCOUNTS

25 RACHAEL, ED AND MATTY

Partnership Appropriation account for the year ended 30 June 20X9

	1 Jul X8 – 31 Dec X8 £	1 Jan X9 – 30 Jun X9 £	Total £
Net profit	110,000	110,000	220,000
Salaries:			
Rachael	9,000	0	9,000
Ed	0	0	0
Matty	18,000	18,000	36,000
Interest on capital:			
Rachael	1,000	0	1,000
Ed	1,000	1,000	2,000
Matty	1,000	1,000	2,000
Profit available for distribution	80,000	90,000	170,000

Profit share:			
Rachael	32,000	0	32,000
Ed	32,000	45,000	77,000
Matty	16,000	45,000	61,000
Total profit distributed	80,000	90,000	170,000

26 NYAH, SHAUNA AND MOLLIE

Partnership Appropriation account for the year ended 31 March 20Y0

	1 Apr X9 – 31 Dec X9 £	1 Jan Y0 – 31 Mar Y0 £	Total £
Net profit	52,500	17,500	70,000
Salaries:			
Nyah	18,750	6,250	25,000
Shauna	14,250	4,750	19,000
Mollie	0	0	0
Interest on capital:			
Nyah	825	275	1,100
Shauna	825	275	1,100
Mollie	825	0	825
Profit available for distribution	17,025	5,950	22,975

	1 Apr X9 – 31 Dec X9 £	1 Jan Y0 – 31 Mar Y0 £	Total £
Profit share:			
Nyah	6,810	4,462	11,272
Shauna	6,810	1,488	8,298
Mollie	3,405	0	3,405
Total profit distributed	17,025	5,950	22,975

27 EDWARD, JAKE AND BELLA

Partnership Appropriation account for the year ended 31 December 20X0

	1 Jan X0 – 30 Apr X0 £	1 May X0 – 31 Dec X0 £	Total £
Net profit	120,000	240,000	360,000
Salaries:			
Edward	10,000	20,000	30,000
Jake	0	0	0
Bella	7,000	14,000	21,000
Interest on capital:			
Edward	1,000	2,000	3,000
Jake	1,000	0	1,000
Bella	1,000	2,000	3,000
Profit available for distribution	100,000	202,000	302,000

Profit share:			
Edward	50,000	121,200	171,200
Jake	20,000	0	20,000
Bella	30,000	80,800	110,800
Total profit distributed	100,000	202,000	302,000

28 GARY, MARK AND ROBBIE

	Gary £	Mark £	Robbie £		Gary £	Mark £	Robbie £
Drawings	34,000	30,000	58,000	Balance b/d	2,000	1,500	250
				Salaries	18,000	0	36,000
Balance c/d	23,000	6,500		Interest	5,000	3,000	3,750
				Profit share	32,000	32,000	16,000
				Balance c/d			2,000
	57,000	36,500	58,000		57,000	36,500	58,000

29 JOHN, JACKIE AND TEGAN

Current accounts

	John £	Jackie £	Tegan £		John £	Jackie £	Tegan £
Balance b/d	750			Balance b/d		1,900	600
Drawings	18,000	35,000	12,750	Salaries	11,000	16,500	0
Balance c/d	20,400	19,390	5,090	Interest	1,900	2,240	2,240
				Profit share	26,250	33,750	15,000
	39,150	54,390	17,840		39,150	54,390	17,840

30 LOUIS, CHERYL AND SIMON

Current accounts

	Louis £	Cheryl £	Simon £		Louis £	Cheryl £	Simon £
Drawings	25,000	10,200	31,000	Balance b/d	3,500	1,800	1,000
Balance c/d	39,500	4,600	9,400	Salaries	30,000	0	21,000
				Interest	1,000	1,000	400
				Profit share	30,000	12,000	18,000
	64,500	14,800	40,400		64,500	14,800	40,400

31 DEREK, JIN AND AHMED

Partnership Appropriation account for the year ended 31 March 20X8:

	£	£
Profit for the year		254,000
Salaries:		
Derek	20,000	
Jin	24,000	
Ahmed	0	
		(44,000)
Interest on capital:		
Derek	8,000	
Jin	7,200	
Ahmed	10,560	
		(25,760)
Interest on drawings:		
Derek	(4,600)	
Jin	(3,800)	
Ahmed	(4,800)	
		13,200
Profit available for distribution		197,440
Profit share:		
Derek	59,232	
Jin	59,232	
Ahmed	78,976	
Total profit distributed		197,440

32 FRED AND JIM

Partnership Appropriation account for the year ended 31 December 20X8:

	£	£
Profit for the year		182,225
Salaries:		
Fred	20,000	
Jim	20,000	
		(40,000)
Interest on capital:		
Fred	2,800	
Jim	6,250	
		(9,050)
Interest on drawings:		
Fred (W)	(2,275)	
Jim	0	
		2,275
Profit available for distribution		135,450

Profit share:		
Fred	67,725	
Jim	67,725	
Total profit distributed		135,450

Working:

Interest on drawings:

1 April 20X8	25,000 × 10% × 9/12 = £1,875
1 September 20X8	12,000 × 10% × 4/12 = £400

UNDERPINNING KNOWLEDGE

33 SHORT FORM QUESTIONS

1 (b)

2 (c)

3 (c)

4 (b)

5 (a)

6   (a)

	Debit	Credit	No change
Sales		✓	
Loan			✓
Non-current assets			✓
Trade receivables	✓		

(b)   A sole trader decides to write off an irrecoverable debt

	Debit	Credit	No change
Trade payables			✓
Inventory			✓
Irrecoverable debt expense	✓		
Trade receivables		✓	

(c)   A sole trader purchases a new computer on credit for use in the business

	Debit	Credit	No change
Discount allowed			✓
Sundry payables		✓	
Non-current assets	✓		
Inventory			✓

Section 3

MOCK ASSESSMENT QUESTIONS

THIS ASSESSMENT CONSISTS OF FIVE TASKS.

COMPLETE ALL TASKS.

TASK 1

You are working on the accounts for a travel business for the year ended 31 October 20X8. There are no credit sales and you have the following additional information below:

Cash and bank summary for the year ended 31 October 20X8

	Cash	Bank		Cash	Bank
	£	£		£	£
Bal b/d	550	7,000	Rent		6,500
Sales	50,000	90,000	Payroll expenses	45,000	
Bank	12,000		Purchases	4,000	11,000
			Payables		30,000
			Advertising	2,000	
			Administration	4,800	
			Cash		12,000
			Light and heat		4,000
			Bal c/d	6,750	33,500
	62,550	**97,000**		**62,550**	**97,000**

The following balances are also available:

Assets and liabilities at:	31 October 20X7	31 October 20X8
Fixtures and fitting – cost	50,000	50,000
Fixtures and fittings – accumulated depreciation	22,000	Not yet available
Inventories	2,500	1,500
Prepayments – rent	2,000	1,000
Payables – Purchases	5,000	4,000
Accruals – Light and heat	700	500

(a) **Calculate the total sales for the year ended 31 October 20X8**

Account name	Amount
	£
Total	

(b) **Prepare the purchases ledger control account for the year ended 31 October 20X8, showing clearly the credit purchases of materials.**

	£		£
Total		Total	

(c) **Calculate the total purchases for the year ended 31 October 20X8**

Account name	Amount
	£
Total	

(d) **Depreciation is calculated at 20% per annum on a reducing balance basis. Calculate the revised accumulated depreciation as at 31 October 20X8.**

Account name	Amount
	£
Total	

(e) **Prepare the rent account for the year ended 31 October 20X8, showing clearly the rent expense for the year**

	£		£
Total		Total	

TASK 2

You are given the following information about a sole trader called Minnie as at 31 March 20X8:
The value of the assets and liabilities were

- Non-current assets at carrying value   £19,175
- Trade receivables   £5,500
- Allowance for doubtful debts   £350
- Prepayments   £250
- Bank overdraft   £575
- Trade payables   £4,775
- Accruals   £375
- Capital   £13,000

There were no other assets or liabilities with the exception of part (a)

(a)   **Calculate the long term loan account balance as at 31 March 20X8**

      £

(b)   On 1 June a piece of equipment was disposed of and the proceeds were received in cash.

      Tick the boxes to show what effect this transaction will have on the balances. You must choose one answer for each line.

Account name	Debit ✓	Credit ✓	No change ✓
Non-current assets at cost			
Accumulated depreciation			
Cash			
Payables			
Depreciation expenses			

(c)   During the year ended 31 March 20X8 a business made sales of £90,000 and operates with a mark-up on cost of 20%.

      Calculate the cost of sales for the year ended 31 March 20X8.

(d)   During the year ended 31 March 20X8 a business made a profit of £20,000 and the proprietor also made drawings of £15,000. The capital balance at 31 March 20X8 was £45,000.

      Calculate the capital of the business as at 31 March 20X7.

TASK 3

You have the following trial balance for a sole trader known as Tanya Trading. All the necessary year-end adjustments have been made.

Trial Balance of Tanya Trading as at 30 June 20X8

	Dr £	Cr £
Capital		40,000
Drawings	15,000	
Fixtures and fittings – cost	50,000	
Fixtures and fittings – accumulated depreciation		27,600
Motor vehicle – cost	10,000	
Motor vehicle – accumulated depreciation		3,000
Closing inventory – statement of financial position	3,480	
Closing inventory – profit or loss		3,480
Prepayments	890	
Accruals		1,000
Payables		6,000
Revenue		140,570
Bank	20,000	
Cash in hand	5,000	
Rent	7,200	
Payroll expenses	42,000	
Purchases	55,000	
Advertising expenses	2,000	
Miscellaneous expenses	1,500	
Depreciation expenses	6,600	
Opening inventory	2,980	
Total	221,650	221,650

(a) **Prepare a statement of profit or loss for the business for the year ended 30 June 20X8**

Statement of profit or loss of Tanya Trading for the year ended 30 June 20X8

	£	£
Revenue		
Cost of goods sold		
Gross profit		
Less:		
Total expenses		
Net profit		

(b) **Indicate where the accruals balance of £1,000 should be shown in the final accounts.**

- Non-current assets
- Long term liabilities
- Current liabilities
- Current assets

TASK 4

You have the following trial balance for a partnership known as the Simpson partnership for the year ended 30 June 20X8. The partners are Peter and Simon.

Simpson partnership Trial Balance as at 30 June 20X8	Dr £	Cr £
Revenue		794,518
Sales returns	5,436	
Purchases	370,215	
Purchases returns		1,447
Opening inventory	41,211	
Payroll expenses	161,326	
General expenses	72,900	
Motor expenses	14,633	
Irrecoverable debts	4,825	
Allowance for doubtful debts		3,425
Motor vehicles – cost	37,400	
Accumulated depreciation – MV		19,160
Fixtures and fittings – cost	46,100	
Accumulated depreciation – F&F		20,855
Capital account – Peter		26,200
Capital account – Simon		37,800
Current account – Peter	15,000	
Current account – Simon	11,000	
Drawings – Peter	18,000	
Drawings – Simon	22,000	
Receivables (Sales ledger) control account	70,367	
Payables (Purchase ledger) control account		25,682
Bank	26,338	
Sales tax		4,529
Closing inventory	54,426	54,426
Loss on disposal	3,870	
Depreciation expense	12,995	
	988,042	988,042

All the year-end adjustments have been made, except for the transfer of profit to current accounts of the partners.

The partnership agreement allows for the following:

- Partners annual salaries

  Peter   £25,000

  Simon   £10,000

- Interest on capital accounts

  3% per annum on the balance at the beginning of the year

- Profit share, effective until 31 March 20X8

  Peter   1/3

  Simon   2/3

- Profit share, effective from 1 April 20X8

  Peter   2/5

  Simon   3/5

- During the year Peter made £18,000 of drawings and Simon £22,000

- Profit for the year ended 30 June 20X8 was £162,980 which accrued evenly during the year

(a) **Prepare the appropriation account for the partnership for the year ended 30 June 20X8.**

Simpson partnership – Appropriation account for the year ended 30 June 20X8			
	1 July 20X7 – 31 Mar 20X8	1 April 20X8 – 30 June 20X8	Total £
Net profit			
Salaries:			
Peter			
Simon			
Interest on capital:			
Peter			
Simon			
Profit available for distribution:			
Profit share:			
Peter			
Simon			

(b) **Update the partners' current accounts for the partnership for the year ended 30 June 20X8. Show clearly the balances carried down on the current accounts.**

	Peter £	Simon £		Peter £	Simon £

TASK 5

Using the information from Task 4, prepare a statement of financial position for the Simpson partnership as at 30 June 20X8.

Simpson partnership – Statement of Financial Position as at 30 June 20X8			
	£	£	£
Non-current assets	Cost	Depreciation	Carrying value
Current assets			
Current liabilities			
Net current assets			
Net assets			
Financed by	Peter	Simon	Total

Section 4

MOCK ASSESSMENT ANSWERS

TASK 1

(a) Calculate the total sales for the year ended 31 October 20X8

Account name	Amount £
Cash	50,000
Bank	90,000
Total	**140,000**

(b) Prepare the purchases ledger control account for the year ended 31 October 20X8, showing clearly the credit purchases of materials.

	£		£
Payments to payables	30,000	Balance b/d	5,000
Balance c/d	4,000	Credit purchases (bal)	29,000
Total	**34,000**	**Total**	**34,000**

(c) Calculate the total purchases for the year ended 31 October 20X8

Account name	Amount £
Credit purchases (part b)	29,000
Cash	4,000
Bank	11,000
Total	**44,000**

(d) Depreciation is calculated at 20% per annum on a reducing balance basis. Calculate the revised accumulated depreciation as at 31 October 20X8.

Account name	Amount £
Accumulated depreciation	22,000
Charge in the year (50,000 – 22,000) × 20%	5,600
Total	27,600

(e) Prepare the rent account for the year ended 31 October 20X8, showing clearly the rent expense for the year

	£		£
Balance b/d	2,000	P&L expense (bal)	7,500
Bank	6,500	Balance c/d – prepayment	1,000
Total	8,500	Total	8,500

TASK 2

(a) Calculate the long term loan account balance as at 31 March 20X8

£5,850

(b) On 1 June 20X8 a piece of equipment was disposed of and the proceeds were received in cash.

Tick the boxes to show what effect this transaction will have on the balances. You must choose one answer for each line.

Account name	Debit ✔	Credit ✔	No change ✔
Non-current assets at cost		✔	
Accumulated depreciation	✔		
Cash	✔		
Payables			✔
Depreciation expenses			✔

(c) During the year ended 31 March 20X8, a business made sales of £90,000 and operates with a mark-up on cost of 20%.

Calculate the cost of sales for the year ended 31 March 20X8.

£90,000 / 1.2 = £75,000

(d) During the year ended 31 March 20X8, a business made a profit of £20,000 and the proprietor also made drawings of £15,000. The capital balance at 31 March 20X8 was £45,000.

Calculate the capital of the business as at 31 March 20X7.

Solution: £45,000 - £20,000 + £15,000 = £40,000

TASK 3

(a) **Prepare a statement of profit or loss for the business for the year ended 30 June 20X8**

Statement of profit or loss for Tanya Trading for the year ended 30 June 20X8

	£	£
Revenue		140,570
Opening inventory	2,980	
Purchases	55,000	
Closing inventory	3,480	
Cost of good sold		54,500
Gross profit		86,070
Less:		
Rent	7,200	
Payroll	42,000	
Advertising	2,000	
Miscellaneous	1,500	
Depreciation	6,600	
Total expenses		59,300
Net profit		26,770

(b) **Indicate where the accruals balance of £1,000 should be shown in the final accounts.**

- Non-current assets
- Long term liabilities
- Current liabilities ✔
- Current assets

TASK 4

(a) Prepare the appropriation account for the partnership for the year ended 30 June 20X8.

Simpson partnership – Appropriation account for the year ended 30 June 20X8			
	1 July 20X7 – 31 March 20X8	1 April 20X8 – 30 June 20X8	Total £
Net profit	122,235	40,745	162,980
Salaries:			
Peter	18,750	6,250	25,000
Simon	7,500	2,500	10,000
Interest on capital:			
Peter	589.5	196.5	786
Simon	850.5	283.5	1,134
Profit available for distribution:	94,545	31,515	126,060
Profit share:			
Peter	31,515	12,606	44,121
Simon	63,030	18,909	81,939

(b) Update the partners' current accounts for the partnership for the year ended 30 June 20X8. Show clearly the balances carried down on the current accounts.

	P £	S £		P £	S £
Balance b/d	15,000	11,000	Salaries	25,000	10,000
Drawings	18,000	22,000	Interest on capital	786	1,134
Balance c/d	36,907	60,073	Profit share	44,121	81,939
	69,907	93,073		69,907	93,073

TASK 5

Prepare a statement of financial position for the Simpson partnership as at 30 June 20X8.

Simpson partnership – Statement of Financial Position as at 30 June 20X8			
	£	£	£
Non-current assets	*Cost*	*Depreciation*	*Carrying value*
Motor vehicles	37,400	19,160	18,240
Fixtures and fittings	46,100	20,855	25,245
			43,485
Current assets			
Inventory		54,426	
Trade receivables (W1)		66,942	
Bank		26,338	
		147,706	
Current liabilities			
Trade payables	25,682		
Sales tax	4,529		
		30,211	
Net current assets			117,495
Net assets			**160,980**
Financed by	*Peter*	*Simon*	*Total*
Capital accounts	26,200	37,800	64,000
Current accounts	36,907	60,073	96,980
			160,980

(W1) Sales ledger control account £70,367 – allowance for doubtful debts £3,425 = £66,942.